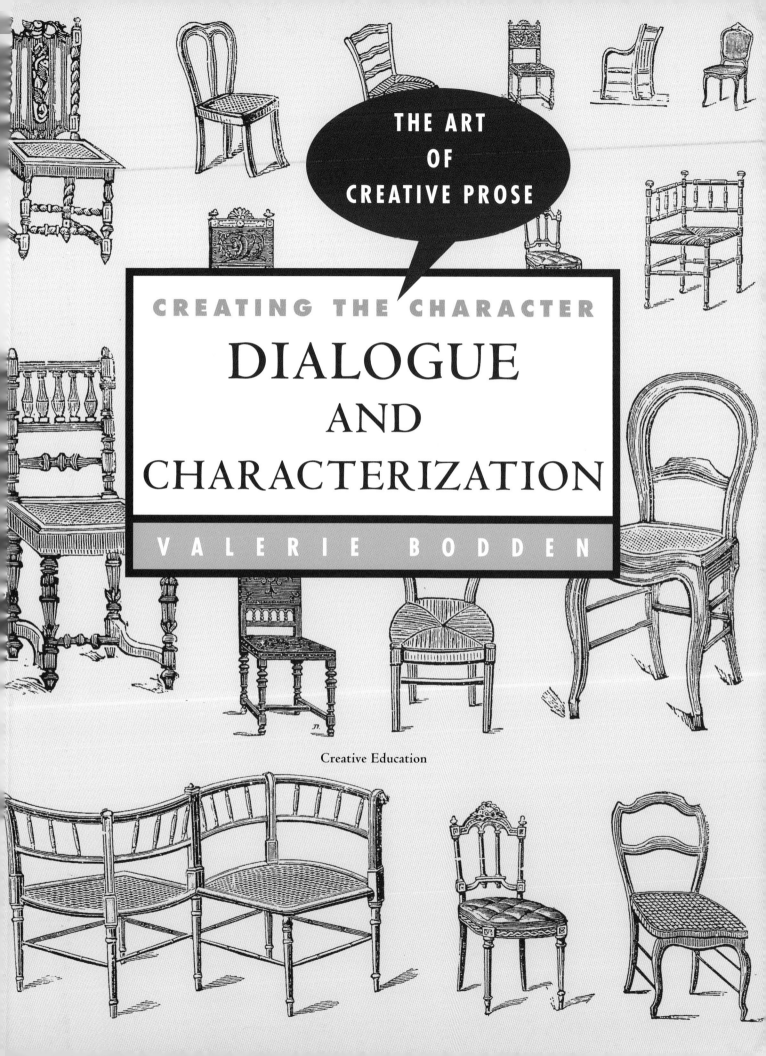

THE ART
OF
CREATIVE PROSE

CREATING THE CHARACTER

DIALOGUE
AND
CHARACTERIZATION

VALERIE BODDEN

Creative Education

Published by Creative Education
P.O. Box 227, Mankato, Minnesota 56002
Creative Education is an imprint of The Creative Company

Design by Stephanie Blumenthal
Production by The Design Lab
Art direction by Rita Marshall
Printed in the United States of America

Photographs by Alamy (Content Mine International, Photos 12), Corbis
(Viviane Moos), Getty Images (Walter Crane, Hulton Archive, Imagno, Robb
Kendrick, Jeff J Mitchell, Pictorial Parade, Sasha, Stock Montage/Stock
Montage, Erik Von Weber), iStockphotos (Oksana Mitiukhina, Emilia Stasiak)

Excerpt on pages 32–33 by J. K. Rowling, *Harry Potter and the Prisoner of Azkaban.*
New York: Scholastic Inc., 1999, pp. 99–100.

Library of Congress Cataloging-in-Publication Data

Bodden, Valerie.
Creating the character: dialogue and characterization / by Valerie Bodden.
p. cm. — (The art of creative prose)
Includes index.
ISBN 978-1-58341-622-8
1. Fiction—Technique. 2. Characters and characteristics in literature.
3. Dialogue in literature. I. Title. II. Series.

PN3383.C4B63 2008
808.3'97—dc22   2007019611

24689753

EVERY DAY, PEOPLE AROUND THE WORLD PICK UP A NOVEL OR SHORT STORY, EAGER TO BE WHISKED AWAY TO ANOTHER REALM. Perhaps that realm is a planet far from Earth, or perhaps it's a medieval castle guarded by a fire-breathing dragon, or maybe it's simply a town not so different from their own. Wherever a work of fiction, or creative **prose**, takes a reader, and whatever happens there, the story is likely to be populated with characters, the **fictional** people who can make a made-up world seem real. Maybe the book you're reading includes a character who reminds you of your happy-go-lucky fifth-grade teacher; maybe another resembles (or is) a pirate on the high seas; and perhaps there's even a character who seems a bit like you.

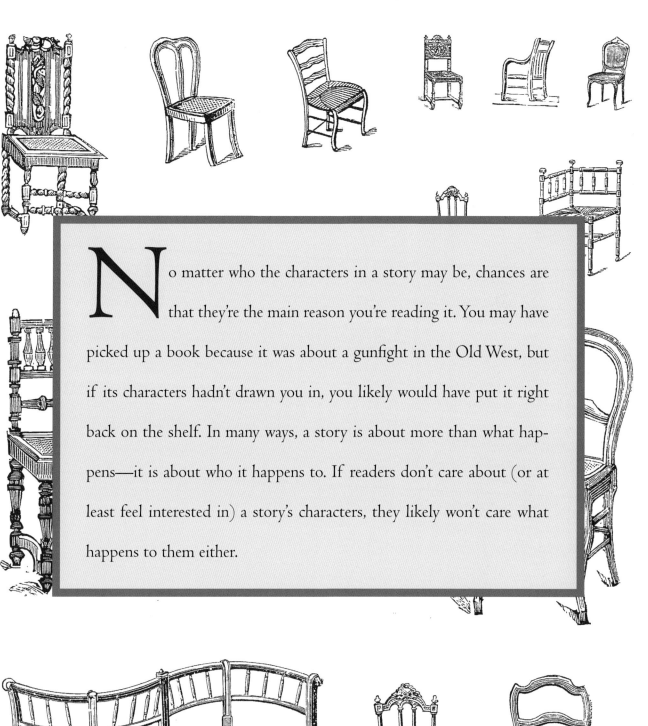

No matter who the characters in a story may be, chances are that they're the main reason you're reading it. You may have picked up a book because it was about a gunfight in the Old West, but if its characters hadn't drawn you in, you likely would have put it right back on the shelf. In many ways, a story is about more than what happens—it is about who it happens to. If readers don't care about (or at least feel interested in) a story's characters, they likely won't care what happens to them either.

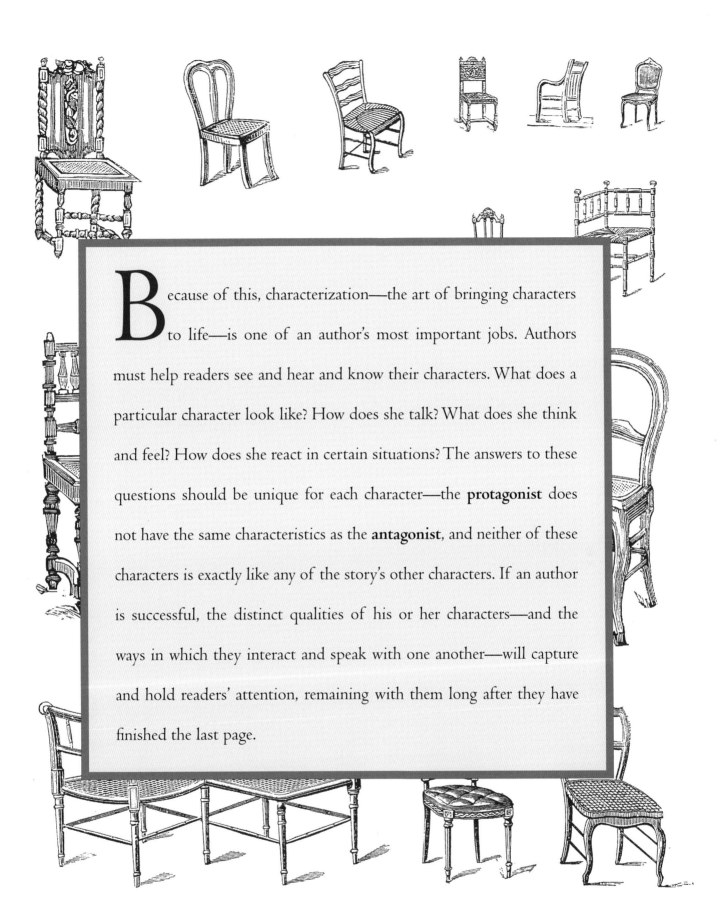

Because of this, characterization—the art of bringing characters to life—is one of an author's most important jobs. Authors must help readers see and hear and know their characters. What does a particular character look like? How does she talk? What does she think and feel? How does she react in certain situations? The answers to these questions should be unique for each character—the **protagonist** does not have the same characteristics as the **antagonist**, and neither of these characters is exactly like any of the story's other characters. If an author is successful, the distinct qualities of his or her characters—and the ways in which they interact and speak with one another—will capture and hold readers' attention, remaining with them long after they have finished the last page.

GETTING TO KNOW THEM

Although some authors simply sit down and begin to write, letting their characters take shape as they go, others feel that the key to creating memorable characters is knowing them inside out before they put their pen to the paper. They plan out not only what their character will do in a story but also what he is like outside of the story: his favorite color, most embarrassing moment, greatest dream, education level, and more. Most likely, not all of these details will make it into the story, but knowing them helps authors know their character better, and knowing their character better helps them make that character more believable to readers.

No matter how much you know about your character when you begin to write, you will generally want to reveal information about him slowly throughout your story. Physical descriptions can help readers picture a character, but most readers today aren't interested in paragraph after paragraph about a character's height, weight, nose shape, and foot size. A few well-chosen details can help a character come to life in a reader's mind—and the reader's imagination will fill in whatever has been left out.

Even more important to characterization than a character's physical appearance is his personality. In order to reveal a character's personality, it is usually most effective to follow the advice, "Show, don't tell." This means that rather than simply telling readers that a character has a certain trait such as optimism, you show the character thinking, saying, or doing something that reveals his optimism—perhaps putting on his swimming trunks and driving to the beach despite the fact that the forecast calls for rain. As you continue to develop your character, you should generally make sure that he stays "in character" throughout the story—for example, the optimist doesn't suddenly do something pessimistic unless he has undergone some sort of change. Readers who encounter a character acting "out of character" may stop believing in him—and your story.

We can see American writer Edith Wharton's skill in revealing character in the following excerpt from *Ethan Frome* (1911), a novel about a rural New Englander who has been hardened by life.

If you know Starkfield, Massachusetts, you know the post-office. If you know the post-office you must have seen Ethan Frome drive up to it, drop the reins on his hollow-backed bay and drag himself across the brick pavement to the white colonnade: and you must have asked who he was.

It was there that, several years ago, I saw him for the first time; and the sight pulled me up sharp. Even then he was the most striking figure in Starkfield, though he was but the ruin of a man. It was not so much his great height that marked him...: it was the careless powerful look he had, in spite of a lameness checking each step like the jerk of a chain. There was something bleak and unapproachable in his face, and he was so stiffened and grizzled that I took him for an old man and was surprised to hear that he was not more than fifty-two. I had this from Harmon Gow....

"He's looked that way ever since he had his smash-up; and that's twenty-four years ago come next February," Harmon threw out between reminiscent pauses.

The "smash-up" it was—I gathered from the same informant—which, besides drawing the red gash across Ethan Frome's forehead, had so shortened and warped his right side that it cost him a visible effort to take the few steps from his buggy to the post-office window....

Every one in Starkfield knew him and gave him a greeting tempered to his own grave mien [manner]; but his taciturnity [reserved nature] was respected and it was only on rare occasions that one of the older men of the place detained him for a word. When this happened he would listen quietly, his blue eyes on the speaker's face, and answer in so low a tone that his words never reached me; then he would climb stiffly into his buggy, gather up the reins in his left hand and drive slowly away in the direction of his farm.

In this excerpt, Wharton has given us—through the eyes of the story's narrator—a vivid description of Ethan Frome. From this description, it is easy for us to picture a man disfigured and aged beyond his years but still imposing and dignified. We can imagine the gash on his forehead and watch him limp, and yet rather than a feeble man, we see a determined one who retains a "careless powerful" look.

Edith Wharton (1862–1937)

Besides relating the key details of Ethan Frome's physical appearance, the narrator also reveals his personality to us. His assertion that if we know Starkfield's post office, we must have seen and asked about Ethan Frome tells us that Ethan stands out from those around him but that he is reserved and unapproachable; just because we must have seen him doesn't mean we would have talked to him. Ethan's personality is further developed by the narrator's account of watching him quietly listen to the men who occasionally talk to him, apparently never revealing any sign of emotion. We begin to see that this man has few close friends—and probably prefers it that way. Because the narrator has also revealed part of Ethan's past to us—the smash-up, or accident—we start to wonder if this event has hardened him or if he has always been an aloof man.

By creating a character that we want to learn more about, Wharton has drawn us into her novel. Believable characters have a way of doing that, so before you sit down to write your next story, try to picture your character coming to life. What would he say to you? Would you be best friends or fierce enemies? Once you know your character, put him on the page, showing readers that he is just who they've always wanted—or dreaded—to meet.

HEROES
HAVE FAULTS, TOO

The main character, or hero, in a work of fiction is called the protagonist. This is the character that readers should ideally care the most about. They should want her to succeed in overcoming whatever obstacles she faces or achieving whatever goal she longs for. Readers don't necessarily have to like her (although it might be easier to draw them into the story if they do), but they should care what happens to her.

Because the protagonist is the character they want readers to root for, beginning writers are often tempted to give their main character only good qualities. They may think that if she is a devoted mother who teaches blind kids and volunteers at a soup kitchen in her spare time, readers will have no choice but to like her. In fact, the opposite may be true—readers may dislike her precisely because she is so perfect. After all, we all have faults. A character with no faults won't seem real, and thus is unlikely to interest real-life readers.

protagonist's faults don't have to be major—perhaps she simply gets cranky when she's hungry—but they can be. In fact, many of the best stories focus on how the protagonist must overcome her flaws—which she may or may not recognize—before she is able to overcome other obstacles or achieve her goals. Early 19th-century English author Jane Austen was a master at revealing a protagonist's flaws. As you read the following excerpt from the novel *Pride and Prejudice* (1813), notice how Elizabeth Bennet's **prejudice** against Mr. Darcy and her feelings for his enemy, Mr. Wickham, prevent her from seeing Darcy in anything but a negative light.

Scene from the 2005 film Pride and Prejudice

Attention, forbearance, patience with Darcy, was injury to Wickham. [Elizabeth] was resolved against any sort of conversation with him, and turned away with a degree of ill humour....

She danced next with an officer, and had the refreshment of talking of Wickham, and of hearing that he was universally liked. When those dances were over she returned to Charlotte Lucas, and was in conversation with her, when she found herself suddenly addressed by Mr. Darcy, who took her so much by surprise in his application for her hand, that, without knowing what she did, she accepted him. He walked away again immediately, and she was left to fret over her own want of presence of mind; Charlotte tried to console her.

'I dare say you will find him very agreeable.'

'Heaven forbid! — That would be the greatest misfortune of all! — To find a man agreeable whom one is determined to hate! — Do not wish me such an evil.'

When the dancing recommenced, however, and Darcy approached to claim her hand, Charlotte could not help cautioning her in a whisper not to be a simpleton and allow her fancy for Wickham to make her appear unpleasant in the eyes of a man of ten times his consequence. Elizabeth made no answer, and took her place in the set, amazed at the dignity to which she was arrived in being allowed to stand opposite to Mr. Darcy, and reading in her neighbours' looks their equal amazement in beholding it. They stood for some time without speaking a word; and she began to imagine that their silence was to last through the two dances, and at first was resolved not to break it; till suddenly fancying that it would be the greater punishment to her partner to oblige him to talk, she made some slight observation on the dance. He replied, and was again silent. After a pause of some minutes she addressed him a second time with —

'It is your turn to say something now, Mr. Darcy. — I talked about the dance, and you ought to make some kind of remark on the size of the room, or the number of couples.'

Even without knowing the basis for Elizabeth's dislike of Darcy (which stems from his declaration earlier in the novel that she is simply "tolerable"), it is clear from this excerpt that no matter how cordial he is or how much he tries to please her, she is determined not to like him. She even says as much herself. Yet, despite Elizabeth's acknowledgement that she wishes to dislike Darcy, she also fails to recognize that it is her own flaw—her own willful prejudice—that prevents her from seeing anything more in him than a disagreeable man. Thus, over and over again, she makes mistakes in judging his character. To be sure, Darcy has his own faults—pride chief among them—but because of her own prejudice, Elizabeth sees only that pride, refusing to acknowledge any proof that Darcy can also be kind and generous.

When, later in the book, Elizabeth receives a letter from Darcy that makes her see how mistaken she has been in her assessment of him, she is mortified, realizing that she has been "blind, partial, prejudiced, absurd." And this realization marks a turning point, not only in the novel, but in Elizabeth herself, who has finally come to recognize her major flaw. Although she must still fight against the urges of that flaw, she eventually overcomes it and realizes that it is precisely Mr. Darcy who will make her happy.

Jane Austen (1775–1817)

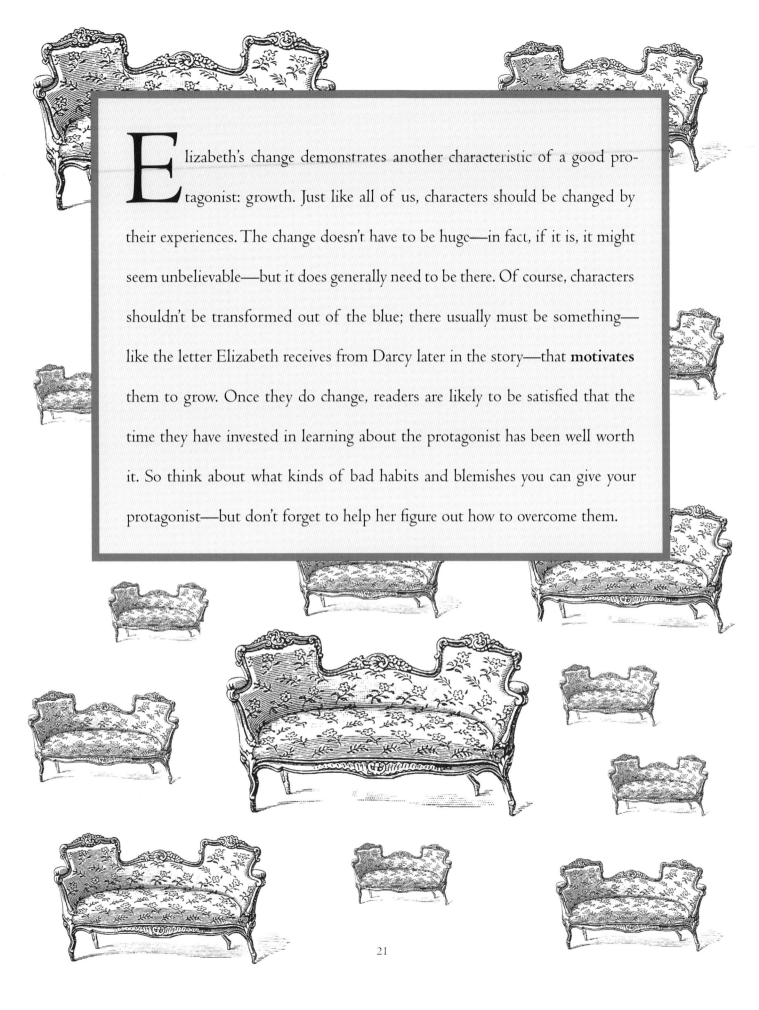

Elizabeth's change demonstrates another characteristic of a good protagonist: growth. Just like all of us, characters should be changed by their experiences. The change doesn't have to be huge—in fact, if it is, it might seem unbelievable—but it does generally need to be there. Of course, characters shouldn't be transformed out of the blue; there usually must be something—like the letter Elizabeth receives from Darcy later in the story—that **motivates** them to grow. Once they do change, readers are likely to be satisfied that the time they have invested in learning about the protagonist has been well worth it. So think about what kinds of bad habits and blemishes you can give your protagonist—but don't forget to help her figure out how to overcome them.

BRINGING OUT THE BAD GUY

As important as the protagonist is to a story, there usually would be no story without the antagonist, or bad guy. This is the character against whom the protagonist struggles. Although the antagonist may be a criminal, he doesn't have to be. The antagonist may simply be someone who wants the opposite of what the protagonist wants. If the protagonist wants to marry the princess, the antagonist is determined to stop him.

Just because the antagonist is the bad guy doesn't mean that he has to be all bad, though. Just like the protagonist, the antagonist should generally be a "round" character, one with a fully developed personality. A character who is pure evil is not only harder for readers to believe in but may also give the story a **melodramatic** feel. Therefore, more often than not, readers should see a villain's good traits as well as his bad ones. Perhaps he is a loving and devoted father but also happens to be a miserly employer who refuses to give the protagonist a raise. Or maybe he's a murderer with a soft spot for animals. Although these good characteristics won't (and shouldn't) necessarily make readers like the antagonist, they will help them to see a real person.

23

Sir Arthur Conan Doyle (1859–1930)

Besides being a fully developed, true-to-life character, the antagonist should usually be at least as strong as the protagonist—and just as motivated to succeed. If he isn't, the protagonist won't achieve much in overcoming him. Or, worse yet, the protagonist might not have any real motive to struggle against him in the first place. In addition to having the desire to oppose the protagonist, the bad guy should be good at what he does. Who's more threatening: a thief who accidentally trips the burglar alarm on his way into the house, or one who hides silently in the closet for hours until everyone is asleep? And who's more intimidating: a boss who stutters and stammers, or one who says in no uncertain terms, "Get back to work"?

British writer Sir Arthur Conan Doyle, the author of the Sherlock Holmes mysteries, knew the importance of a competent, powerful opponent. In the short story "The Adventure of the Final Problem" (1892), the narrator, Watson, recounts Sherlock Holmes's description of Professor Moriarty, the man who ultimately brings Holmes to his death. As you read the following excerpt, note the characteristics that make Moriarty an exceptionally powerful foe.

"[Professor Moriarty]

pervades London, and no one has heard of him. That's what
puts him on a pinnacle in the records of crime. I tell you Watson,
in all seriousness, that if I could beat that man, if I could free
society of him, I should feel that my own career had
reached its summit, and I should be prepared to
turn to some more placid line in life.... But I could
not rest, Watson, I could not sit quiet in my chair, if
I thought that such a man as Professor Moriarty were
walking the streets of London unchallenged."

"What has he done then?"

"His career has been an extraordinary one.
He is a man of good birth and excellent education,
endowed by nature with a phenomenal mathematical faculty. At the age of twenty-one he wrote a

treatise upon the binomial theorem, which has had a European vogue. On the strength
of it he won the mathematical chair at one of our smaller universities, and had, to all
appearances, a most brilliant career before him. But the man had hereditary tendencies of
the most diabolical kind. A criminal strain ran in his blood, which, instead of being modi-
fied, was increased and rendered infinitely more dangerous by his extraordinary mental
powers. Dark rumours gathered round him in the university town, and eventually
he was compelled to resign his chair and to come down to London....

"He is the Napoleon of crime, Watson. He is the organizer of half that is evil
and of nearly all that is undetected in this great city. He is a genius, a philoso-
pher, an abstract thinker. He has a brain of the first order....

"You know my powers, my dear Watson, and yet at the end of three months
I was forced to confess that I had at last met an antagonist who was my intel-
lectual equal. My horror at his crimes was lost in my admiration at his skill....

"His soft, precise fashion of speech leaves a conviction of sincerity which
a mere bully could not produce."

Although we see little more of Professor Moriarty than what Holmes tells Watson, we know that he is a villain of the highest order. But Moriarty isn't only evil; he is also smart. And his intelligence, in addition to helping to round out his character, makes him more of a threat to the brilliant Sherlock Holmes. This criminal is likely to anticipate each of Holmes's next moves, making any action against him particularly dangerous.

Although Holmes admires Moriarty's intellect and skill—or perhaps *because* he does—he finds the professor more threatening than he would any "mere bully." Moriarty's "soft, precise fashion of speech" leaves Holmes unsettled, convinced that this criminal not only is able to do what he says, but that he is capable of following through. To have gone undiscovered in London for so long, Moriarty must be not only competent, but a mastermind. People throughout London have probably talked to him without ever suspecting his criminal nature. Think about the "quiet-neighbor-next-door" criminals who no one would ever have thought capable of murder. Like Professor Moriarty, their nearness—their realness—makes them more formidable.

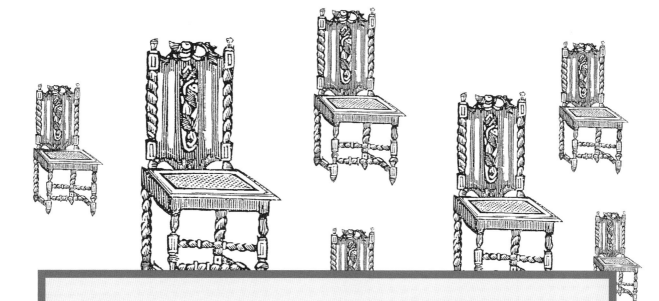

Although the antagonist of a story won't necessarily appear on every page—after all, the story is really about the protagonist—his presence must hover over almost every sentence. Readers should rarely, if ever, be allowed to forget about the looming challenge this character represents. Remember this when you're creating your bad guy, and you just might come up with an antagonist capable of matching wits with the great Sherlock Holmes—or, better yet, your own worthy protagonist!

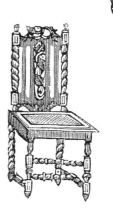

MINOR CHARACTERS

ARE IMPORTANT, TOO

Every day, we come across people who might be considered "minor characters" in our lives. Perhaps it is the clerk at the grocery store or the receptionist at the dentist's office. Although these people may seem to be of little consequence to us, they still have an impact—however small—on our lives. The same is true of minor characters in a work of fiction. These characters may either help or hamper the protagonist in some small way. Perhaps they are sent to deliver a message that will aid the protagonist in reaching her goal. Or maybe they pose an obstacle, delaying the protagonist at a critical juncture.

Whatever effect they have on the protagonist, a story's minor characters should be just as believable as its main characters. Although they are unlikely to be as developed as the main characters, minor characters should generally be individuals, not **stereotypes**. Stereotypes include the dumb blond, the roughneck truck driver, and the country bumpkin. Such characters usually add little interest to a story, so rather than sticking with these **clichés**, think about what differentiates your minor character from the stereotype. Maybe you create an Ivy League-educated blond, a gospel-singing truck driver, or a high-fashion designer living in the country. Whether they appear one time or many in the course of the story, minor characters should have unique quirks and personality traits that make them memorable.

The fantasy world that **contemporary** British author J. K. Rowling has created in her *Harry Potter* books is peppered with memorable minor characters. In the following excerpt from *Harry Potter and the Prisoner of Azkaban* (1999), the boy wizard Harry and his friends encounter a talking, moving portrait of a knight named Sir Cadogan. As you read the excerpt, think about Sir Cadogan's unique traits. What does his purpose in the story seem to be?

Harry was watching the painting. A fat, dapple-gray pony had just ambled onto the grass and was grazing nonchalantly. Harry was used to the subjects of Hogwarts paintings moving around and leaving their frames to visit one another, but he always enjoyed watching it. A moment later, a short, squat knight in a suit of armor clanked into the picture after his pony. By the look of the grass stains on his metal knees, he had just fallen off.

"Aha!" he yelled, seeing Harry, Ron, and Hermione. "What villains are these, that trespass upon my private lands! Come to scorn at my fall, perchance? Draw, you knaves, you dogs!"

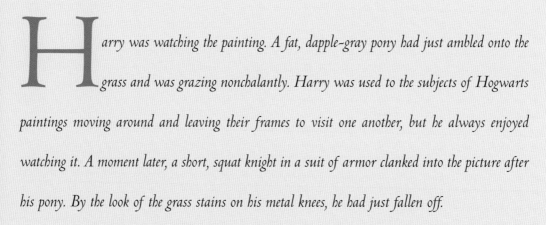

They watched in astonishment as the little knight tugged his sword out of its scabbard and began brandishing it violently, hopping up and down in rage. But the sword was too long for him; a particularly wild swing made him overbalance, and he landed face-down in the grass.

"Are you all right?" said Harry, moving closer to the picture.

"Get back, you scurvy braggart! Back, you rogue!"

The knight seized his sword again and used it to push himself back up, but the blade sank deeply into the grass and, though he pulled with all his might, he couldn't get it out again. Finally, he had to flop back down onto the grass and push up his visor to mop his sweating face.

"Listen," said Harry, taking advantage of the knight's exhaustion, "we're looking for the North Tower. You don't know the way, do you?"

"A quest!" The knight's rage seemed to vanish instantly. He clanked to his feet and shouted, "Come follow me, dear friends, and we shall find our goal, or else shall perish bravely in the charge!"

He gave the sword another fruitless tug, tried and failed to mount the fat pony, gave up, and cried, "On foot then, good sirs and gentle lady! On! On!"

And he ran, clanking loudly, into the left side of the frame and out of sight.

They hurried after him along the corridor, following the sound of his armor. Every now and then they spotted him running through a picture ahead.

Certainly, Rowling could have told this story without the aid of Sir Cadogan, but introducing this minor character accomplishes several tasks. To begin with, Sir Cadogan brings a bit of comic relief to the story. Although Sir Cadogan could have come across as a stereotypical knight in his eagerness to vanquish foes and complete adventurous **quests**, he is individualized—and made humorous—by his incompetence. Evidently, this knight was not created to do battle or mount his steed—which makes sense given that he's a picture.

In addition to injecting humor into the story, Sir Cadogan also shows us a bit more about the magical world of Hogwarts, where Harry and his friends go to school. Rather than simply writing that the pictures could move and talk, Rowling shows us a picture doing so. As Sir Cadogan runs from frame to frame, he also accomplishes another task: moving the plot forward. It is he who gets Harry and his friends to the North Tower, where their next class—and a prediction of Harry's death—await. Although Harry and his friends could simply have walked to the North Tower on their own (had they not gotten lost), the introduction of Sir Cadogan makes this a much more interesting journey.

Although Sir Cadogan shows up only a couple of times in the story, our brief introduction to him is memorable. We have no reason to believe at the end of the story that he is any different from when we last encountered him—and that's fine. Minor characters rarely undergo a change during the course of a story. Their job is to show up—however briefly—play their part in assisting or obstructing the protagonist, and disappear again—gone but not forgotten. So the next time you're at the store, think about how the clerk has helped (with a cheerful word) or hindered (with slow service) your life. Does your protagonist need someone like that in her life?

J. K. Rowling (1965–)

TALKING IT OVER

As a writer, one of your most useful characterization tools is dialogue, or conversations between two or more characters. By listening to a character talk, readers can often learn more about his education level, status in society, relationships with others, and attitudes. A character who says, "I swear I didn't do it" obviously has a different background than one who says, "How dare you suggest that I am capable of such treachery," and this character is in turn different from the one who says, "I ain't done nothin'."

Of course, just as no two people in the real world speak in exactly the same way—even if they come from similar backgrounds—ideally, no two characters in a story should have the exact same speech patterns, either. Just as you can probably easily identify your mom's voice even without seeing her, it should be easy for readers to distinguish who is talking simply by what they say and the way in which they say it.

"How dare you suggest that I am capable of such treachery."

"I swear I didn't do it."

In order to write realistic dialogue, it is helpful to listen in on the conversations around you. In doing so, you'll notice that people rarely speak in complete, smooth sentences. Most people's speech is characterized by pauses, **sentence fragments**, incomplete thoughts, and informal **grammar**. Thus, a character who makes long, flowery speeches is likely to sound awkward or unbelievable. At the same time, though, dialogue shouldn't imitate real-life conversations **verbatim**. A written conversation that included all of the "ums," "uhs," and "you know's" that populate most people's speech would make for a tedious read.

In addition, pleasantries such as "Hi, how are you doing?" are usually unnecessary in prose dialogue, which should move the story forward rather than bring the action to a standstill. The short novel *Washington Square* (1881) by American-born author Henry James is largely driven by dialogue. In the excerpt that follows, Catherine tells Morris, the young man she wishes to marry, that her father will disinherit her if the two wed.

"I ain't done nothin'."

It was quite on [Catherine's] conscience to deliver this message, and had the mission been ten times more painful, she would have as scrupulously performed it. "He told me to tell you—to tell you very distinctly, and directly from himself—that if I marry without his consent, I shall not inherit a penny of his fortune. He made a great point of this. He seemed to think—he seemed to think—"

Morris flushed, as any young man of spirit might have flushed at an imputation of baseness [accusation of greediness]. "What did he seem to think?"

"That it would make a difference."

"It will make a difference—in many things. We shall be of many thousands of dollars the poorer; and that is a great difference. But it will make none in my affection."

"We shall not want the money," said Catherine; "for you know I have a good deal myself."

"Yes, my dear girl, I know you have something. And he can't touch that."

"He would never," said Catherine. "My mother left it to me."

Morris was silent awhile. "He was very positive about this, was he?" he asked at last. "He thought such a message would annoy me terribly, and make me throw off the mask, eh?"

"I don't know what he thought," said Catherine, sadly.

"Please tell him that I care for his message as much as for that!" and Morris snapped his fingers sonorously [loudly].

"I don't think I could tell him that."

"Do you know you sometimes disappoint me," said Morris.

"I should think I might. I disappoint every one—father and Aunt Penniman."

"Well, it doesn't matter with me, because I am fonder of you than they are."

"Yes, Morris," said the girl, with her imagination—what there was of it—swimming in this happy truth....

"Is it your belief that he will stick to it—stick to it forever—to this idea of disinheriting you?—that your goodness and patience will never wear out his cruelty?"

"The trouble is that if I marry you he will think I am not good. He will think that a proof."

Even after reading only this short excerpt, it is easy to pick out the defining characteristics of each of these characters. Catherine is a woman torn between the two men in her life—her father and Morris. She is afraid to defy the one but has no desire to leave the other and wants only to please both. Morris is a strong, passionate man who claims to be terribly insulted by the insinuation that he is interested in Catherine only for her fortune; yet we can't help feeling that he does have more than a passing interest in her money. James could simply have told us these things, of course, but reading Catherine's and Morris's words for ourselves gives us a much stronger impression of these characters.

Notice that James uses very few "he said" or "she said" tags in this dialogue. They are unnecessary, as it is clear which character is speaking at any given moment. (Although had the **scene** involved more than just two characters, "said" tags would have been essential.) Notice also that Catherine and Morris occasionally speak in sentence fragments or break off in the middle of a thought, which helps the dialogue to feel more realistic. And, as they talk, Catherine and Morris continue to move and think, sometimes revealing as much through their nonverbal communication—such as Morris's snap—as through what they say.

Henry James (1843–1916)

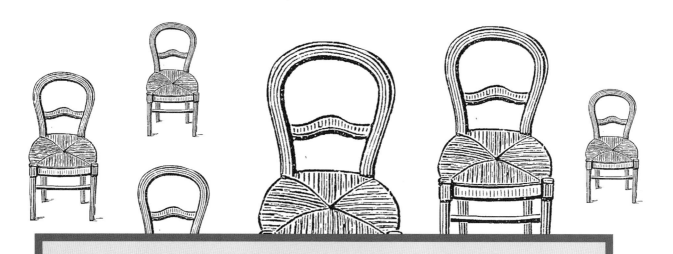

W hen you know your characters inside out—know what they would say or do or think at any given moment—you know them well enough to share them with your readers. Remember that your characters *are* the story. Without them, there would be no one for the story to happen to. So think about what makes your good guy (or gal) bad, your bad guy good, and your little guys important. Then show your readers that your characters are fictional versions of the people they see every day—their neighbors, their friends, and maybe even themselves!

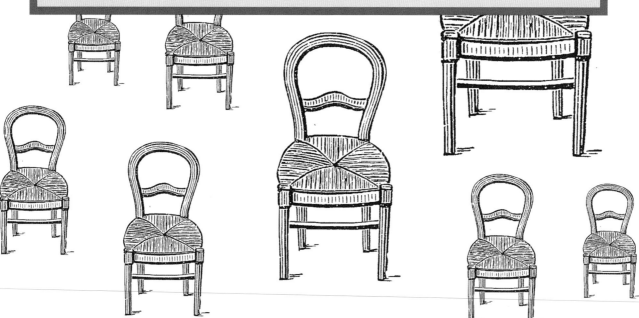

As with most things in life, the best way to become a good writer is to practice. The exercises below—along with careful observation of the world around you—will help you get started in creating realistic characters and dialogue.

THE CHARACTER SKETCH In order to get to know your character before you start to write about him or her, make a list of everything you can think of about that character. In addition to the basics such as name, age, height, and hair color, consider the character's nationality, education, family, and home. Also include information that would help to reveal his or her personality: likes and dislikes, dreams and ambitions, emotions and habits. After you have finished, look back over your list and decide which traits are most important in this character. Then, write a paragraph or two revealing these traits by showing rather than telling. For example, if one of the character's dreams is to become a writer, you could show his or her excitement at having a story published in the school newspaper.

A WELL-ROUNDED CHARACTER Think about your favorite fictional protagonist. Make a list of all the things you can remember about him or her, both good and bad. Now go back and reread the short story or novel in which that character appears. As you read, make another list, again of the character's good and bad traits, but this time based on what you read rather than what you remember. When you're done, compare your lists. How close are they to one another? Did you remember more of the protagonist's good traits or bad? After reading the work again, do you think this character is well-rounded? Why or why not?

THE BAD GUY'S TURN While you will most likely tell your story from the point of view of your protagonist or someone who is sympathetic to your protagonist, it doesn't hurt to think about things from the bad guy's point of view. In order to get to know your antagonist better, write a short scene from his or her point of view. The plot doesn't need to be complicated—perhaps he or she bullied someone on the bus or stole a cookie from a gas station. As you write, remember that your antagonist is unlikely to be completely bad, and show a detail or two that reveals one of his or her better traits. At the same time, you needn't make the antagonist likeable; after all, if readers like him or her, they may not root as hard for the good guy.

DON'T FORGET THE LITTLE PEOPLE Make a list of the minor characters in your life. They may be people you see in passing every day, or they may be people you've seen only once in your life. After each person's name or identity, write a few characteristics that you remember about him or her. Now, write a short story in which you are the protagonist and you encounter three of these characters. Try to show readers that these are real people, not stereotypes. And don't have them simply pass in and out of a scene without doing anything. They should have some influence—whether positive or negative—on your behavior or life.

MAKING IT SOUND REAL Write a short dialogue in which two characters have a heated argument. You can include some of their nonverbal actions, but the scene should rely mainly on dialogue. When you have finished writing your scene, get a friend to read it out loud with you. Record yourselves as you read, then play the tape back and think about whether or not the dialogue sounds real. Does each character come through with a different voice? Do the characters speak in short, sometimes choppy sentences? Can you tell what emotions they are feeling? If the answer to any of these questions is no, go back and rework your dialogue until it sounds real.

GLOSSARY

antagonist: the character in a work of fiction who opposes the main character

clichés: images and phrases that have been overused and are no longer new

contemporary: of the present time

fictional: not real; part of an imaginary story

grammar: the rules that govern language and the correct formation of sentences

melodramatic: overdone writing that is more emotional or dramatic than the scene calls for

motivates: provides a strong reason to take action

prejudice: a preformed, unfavorable opinion of someone or something founded on incomplete information or unreasonable feelings

prose: speech or writing that is not poetry, but sounds more like everyday speech

protagonist: the main character in a work of fiction

quests: long and difficult journeys or adventures in search of something

scene: a single episode in a short story or novel

sentence fragments: incomplete sentences that are lacking some part of speech such as the subject or the verb

stereotypes: characters who fit an oversimplified idea about a group of people or a type of person

verbatim: in the exact same words

BIBLIOGRAPHY

Conrad, Barnaby. *The Complete Guide to Writing Fiction*. Cincinnati, Ohio: Writer's Digest Books, 1990.

Lyon, Elizabeth. *A Writer's Guide to Fiction*. New York: Perigee, 2004.

Naylor, Phyllis Reynolds. *The Craft of Writing the Novel*. Boston: The Writer, 1989.

Phillips, Kathleen. *How to Write a Story*. New York: Franklin Watts, 1995.

Plagemann, Bentz. *How to Write a Story*. New York: Lothrop, Lee & Shepard, 1971.

Rubie, Peter. *The Elements of Storytelling*. New York: John Wiley & Sons, 1996.

Sorenson, Sharon. *How to Write Short Stories*. New York: Macmillan, 1998.

FURTHER READING

Austen, Jane. *Pride and Prejudice*. New York: Penguin Books, 1985.

Doyle, Sir Arthur Conan. *Sherlock Holmes: The Complete Novels and Stories*. Vol. I. New York: Bantam Books, 1986.

James, Henry. *The Henry James Reader*. Compiled by Leon Edel. New York: Charles Scribner's Sons, 1965.

Rowling, J. K. *Harry Potter and the Prisoner of Azkaban*. New York: Scholastic, 1999.

Wharton, Edith. *Ethan Frome*. New York: Signet Classic, 2000.